POSTCARD, 1908

COPYRIGHT
'08.

H.C. WESTERHOUSE,

Paul Ecke Ranch

Poinsettias

the December flower

Poinsettias

the December flower

MYTH & LEGEND ~ HISTORY & BOTANICAL FACT

CHRISTINE ANDERSON & TERRY TISCHER

WATERS EDGE PRESS
California

Thanks Tom!

PUBLISHER'S CATALOGING-IN-PUBLICATION
(Provided by Quality Books, Inc.)
Anderson, Christine, 1945-
Poinsettias, the December flower : myth and legend-- history and botanical fact /
Christine Anderson & Terry Tischer. -- 1st ed.
p.cm.
Includes bibliographical references and index.
Preassigned LCCN: 96-60667
ISBN: 0-965-6224-9-5
1. Poinsettias. 2. Christmas decorations. 3. Poinsettias--Mythology. 4. Flowers in art.
I. Tischer, Terry. II. Title.
SF413.P63A63 1998   583'.95
QBI97-647
Design Consultants: Catherine Flanders, Al Stutrud
Type: Bernhard Modern BT & Shelly Allegro BT

WATERS EDGE PRESS
98 Main Street #527 Tiburon, CA 94920
415-435-2837
FAX: 415-435-2404
email: wtrsedgeps@aol.com

First Edition

Printed and bound in Hong Kong
First Printing June 1997
8 7 6 5 4 3 2

Poinsettia. *"California's Christmas Flower."*

POSTCARD, 1909.

Table of Contents

> *"Christmas is not a time or season,
> but a state of mind."*
> CALVIN COOLIDGE (1872-1933)

No doubt about it. A row of potted poinsettias perched in a windowsill can put a passerby into a holiday mood. So how did poinsettias, dismissed by 19th century botanists as a lowly *weed,* become such a popular, universally recognizable symbol of Christmas?

Although the ancient Aztecs prized poinsettias for their medicinal, commercial and religious value, the plants probably would have languished in obscurity were it not for Joel Poinsett, the first United States Ambassador to Mexico. An avid amateur botanist, he chanced upon the tall, fiery red wildflower in December, 1828 while roaming the countryside. Enchanted by the alluring blooms, Poinsett shipped cuttings back to his greenhouse in South Carolina. The rest...is history. All who saw the exotic-looking plant were bewitched by its unique beauty, and within a decade poinsettias had taken their place alongside holly and mistletoe as a Yuletide tradition.

Today, the horticultural wonders are big business: each year 150 million carefully cultivated potted poinsettias, in every size, shape and color imaginable, are sold in more than 50 countries. What's more, their distinctive profile graces a plethora of holiday merchandise, from napkins to neckties.

Lyons Ltd. Antique Prints

HAND-COLORED ENGLISH ENGRAVING, CIRCA 1820.

Roots

"Give fools their gold, and
knaves their power;
Let fortune's bubbles rise and fall;
Who sows a field, or
trains a flower,
Or plants a tree, is more than all."

JOHN GREENLEAF WHITTIER (1807-1892)

All in the Family

Poinsettias belong to the *Euphorbiaceae* family, a gigantic, extraordinarily diverse clan containing more than 8,000 species of herbs, shrubs, perennials, biennials, annuals, succulents and trees. The family's roots can be traced to East Africa 800 million years ago. Thanks to *Euphorbiaceae's* versatility (it's been used as everything from a source of latex, to fish poison, religious fetishes and medicine), ancient nomadic tribes took cuttings and transplanted them in hundreds of new geographical areas. Today, except for mountainous and polar regions, the hearty *Euphorbiaceae* thrives in every corner of the globe.

Botanists group plants that share the same broad similarities in a hierarchical system to make identification easier. Poinsettias are members of the:

KINGDOM: *Plantae*

DIVISION: *Magnoliophyta*

CLASS: *Magnoliopsida*

ORDER: *Euphorbiales*

FAMILY: *Euphorbiaceae*

GENUS: *Euphorbia*

SPECIES: *Pulcherrima*

California Academy of Sciences

THE *Euphorbiaceae* FAMILY BY MEYER, 1902.

IN THE WILD, POINSETTIAS ARE LEGGY, 8 TO 12-FOOT-TALL SHRUBS WITH STIFF, CANE-LIKE BRANCHES, AND COARSE, BRIGHT GREEN LEAVES MEASURING 6 TO 8 INCHES ACROSS. THEIR BRILLIANT RED COLOR LASTS FROM THE FIRST OF NOVEMBER THROUGH THE END OF JANUARY, AND UNLIKE THEIR HOT HOUSE RELATIVES, MANY ARE DECIDUOUS, SO THEY DROP THEIR LEAVES IN WINTER.

That Milky White Sap

The genus *Euphorbia* was first recognized by Linnaeus (1707-1778), the Swedish botanist who developed the system to classify all life forms.

Although *Euphorbia are* wildly different in appearance (from slender, willowy shrubs to fat little cactus look-alikes), nearly all 1,600 species ooze a milky white sap when cut. This is thought to be an adaptation to the hot, dry South American climate where the genus originated 30 million years ago.

In some, the sap is irritating to the skin or even poisonous, while the sticky liquid in others can be extracted and made into market-able products. For example, castor oil is from an *African Euphorbia*, rubber is harvested from a tropical *American Euphorbia*, and a furni-ture polish called *tung oil* is made from the opaque liquid of a *Chinese Euphorbia*.

KISSING COUSIN: *Euphorbia milii splendens*, *BOTANICAL MAGAZINE*, 1829.

Paul Ecke Ranch, Encinitas, California

POINSETTIAS' FLOWERS, KNOWN AS _cyathia_.

Beauty Secrets

See those tiny, inconspicuous yellow and green clusters? Those are flowers! Poinsettias, like other _Euphorbia_ have a single, petal-less female flower surrounded by male flowers enclosed in a cup-shaped structure, called _cyathium_. The showy blaze of color that stains the plants' leaves are actually _bracts_. This beauty secret - _bracts_ so brightly-colored, large and impressive they are often mistaken for flowers - is shared by bougainvillea and dogwoods. The colorful _bracts_, like a flower's petals, lure insects into the _cyathia_ for reproductive purposes.

Susan's Store Room

Glass
Paperweight,
circa 1945.

AN UNKNOWN AZTEC ARTIST DEPICTS MONTEZUMA IN 1502 REGALLY ATTIRED IN CEREMONIAL ROBES, HIS NOSE PIERCED WITH A BONE IN PREPARATION FOR HIS ELEVATION TO THE THRONE, RECEIVING THE CROWN FROM A ROYAL SUBJECT. MONTEZUMA IMPORTED POINSETTIAS INTO HIS EMPIRE.

THE AZTECS

Poinsettias, called *cuetlaxochitle* by the ancient Aztecs, were a highly-prized commodity in the Valley of Mexico from the 14th through the 16th century:

- HEALERS AND MEDICINE MEN COUNTED ON THE MILKY WHITE SAP TO CONTROL FEVERS.

- CLOTHING MERCHANTS BREWED THE BRACTS TO MAKE A REDDISH-PURPLE COTTON FABRIC DYE.

- AND PRIESTS USED IT IN CEREMONY BECAUSE THE FIERY RED COLOR WAS THE SYMBOL OF PURITY.

Both Nezahualcoyotl (1410- 1472), the renowned ruler who molded Tenochtitlan (now Mexico City) from a swamp into an imposing imperial city, and Montezuma (1480-1520), the last of the great Aztec warrior-kings, were forced to import poinsettias, as they could not be grown in the high altitude of the capital city. So when crowds, often numbering 50,000, gathered in the open air market each day to barter for beans, maize and other staples, it was commonplace to spy caravans laden with the exotic *cuetlaxochitle* as well.

A "Virtuous" Plant...

THE FIRST WRITTEN MENTION of *Euphorbia* was in connection with Hippocrates' (BC 469-399) study of medicine. Prior to the 1600s, the only plants considered worthy of note were those with medicinal or utilitarian value. Even botanical drawings and woodcuts memorialized a plant's "virtues" rather than its physical characteristics.

EUROPEAN PHYSICIANS believing the more peculiar the plant, the greater its potential to heal, were enthusiastic about the medicinal potential for *Euphorbia* because of its strange, copious white sap. Doctors claimed it could improve vision, and was an effective remedy against lethargy and snake bites.

"GUM EUPHORBIUM" from the Canary Islands and Morocco was so immensely popular as a remedy for chronic human and animal diseases, ships traveled from the Netherlands to buy the dried sap from the Tamil, Singhalese, Hindu and Balinese in order to sell it in the medical marketplaces of Amsterdam, Antwerp and London during the 1500s.

WITCH DOCTORS in Venezuela, Brazil and Peru in pre-Columbian times often included *Euphorbia* in their herbal medicine kit. *Euphorbia antisyphilitica,* for example, was considered a particularly valuable cure for syphilis.

Lyons Ltd. Antique Prints

...Or Just a Weed?

WHAT IS A WEED?

IT DEPENDS ON WHO ANSWERS THE QUESTION. MOST 19TH CENTURY BOTANISTS DISMISSED POINSETTIAS AS A *LOWLY WEED*.

"...a plant out of place."

W. J. BEAL, WEED SPECIALIST

"A plant that grows so luxuriantly or plentifully that it chokes out all other plants that possess more valuable...properties."

W. E. BRENCHLEY, WEED EXPERT

"A plant growing where it is not desired."

THE TERMINOLOGY COMMITTEE OF THE WEED SOCIETY OF AMERICA

"...plant(s) not valued for use or beauty, growing wild and rank... hindering the growth of superior vegetation."

THE OXFORD ENGLISH DICTIONARY

IT IS, HOWEVER, RALPH WALDO EMERSON'S DEFINITION OF A WEED AS:

"a plant whose virtues have not yet been discovered,"

WHICH BEST DESCRIBES POINSETTIAS.

© *Weeds* by Mea Allen, The Viking Press. Reprinted with permission.

CHROMOLITHOGRAPH OF *poinsettia pulcherrima plerussima*, 1870.

What's in a Name?

Poinsettia
A beautiful Flower of California

Blooming in the winter-time—
In this warm and sun kissed clime,
Poinsettia, rich and red—
Crimson glory round does shed!

POSTCARD, 1901.

Poinsettia,
THE POPULAR NAME

Although plant names often reflect the color, form, leaf structure or the geographical region where a plant grows or is discovered, names sometimes honor a person. Such was the case with poinsettias. When the Christmas novelty began to gain popularity, William H. Prescott, a respected historian and gardener, was asked to rename it (*Euphorbia pulcherrima* just didn't have the right ring). As chance would have it, Prescott had just published *Conquest of Mexico*, which included the facts surrounding Joel Poinsett's "discovery" of the plant. So, to honor Poinsett's horticultural and diplomatic achievements he christened the holiday beauty *poinsettia*.

Euphorbiaceae,
THE FAMILY NAME

One of the 20,000 scientific "facts" Pliny (AD 23-79), the Roman historian and scientific authority, included in his encyclopedia *Historia Naturalis* was how *Euphorbiaceae* got its name:

"In the age...of our fathers, King Juba (of Mauretania) discovered a plant to which he gave the name Euphorbea, calling it after his own physician Euphorbus..."

Euphorbia Pulcherrima,
THE BOTANICAL NAME

Karl Ludwig Wilenow, a distinguished German botanist, gave the plants their botanical name in 1833 after one crept into his greenhouse through a crack in the wall. Recognizing it as a *Euphorbia* and impressed by its distinctive coloring, he dubbed the intruder *pulcherrima*, meaning "very beautiful" *Euphorbia*.

Spurge,
THE COMMON NAME

Both the family *Euphorbiaceae* and the genus *Euphorbia* are commonly known as *spurge,* a derivation of the word *expurgate* meaning to purge, cleanse or purify. The plants were given this name after physicians in the 1500s discovered that small doses of the dried sap proved a powerful laxative.

Postcard, 1910.

What *is* the proper pronunciation?

Is it poyn-SEHT-ee-uh *or* poyn-SEHT-uh? According to the dictionary it's your choice. Both are correct.

The East Coast pronunciation, poin-SEHT-er, *is* incorrect, but it gave readers of *The New Yorker* a chuckle when the following appeared in the January, 1947 issue:

> "Memo to Dog Lovers: Sal's Flower Shop, at 1491 Lexington Avenue, has been advertising a full line of cut flowers and *point setters*."

Nicknames

Poinsettias have also answered to:

flores de la noche buena
(Flowers of the Holy Night)

fire flower

cuetlaxochitle

flame leaf

lobster flower

and even RATWEED!

Merry Christmas

May your heart beat
To the Christmas Chime,
May your home be a treat
To Joy all the time.

Postcard, 1914.

Myth & Legend

"Myth is the secret opening
through which
the inexhaustible energies of the
cosmos pour...
the very dreams that blister sleep,
boil up from the basic,
magic ring of myth."

PROLOGUE, THE HERO WITH A THOUSAND FACES, 1949

JOSEPH CAMPBELL (1904-1987)

J OEL ROBERTS POINSETT would have laughed out loud had someone suggested he would one day be famous for *finding a flower*. Born in Charleston, South Carolina, young Joel, the brilliant only son of a doctor, was given a classical education in England. Fascinated with military science, he determined to become a soldier. But when his father learned of this ambition, Joel was promptly transferred to the medical school at the University of Edinburgh.

I n 1800, ill health forced Poinsett to return to South Carolina where he abandoned medicine to study law. When his father died, he inherited a modest fortune, which allowed him to spend the next 10 years traveling throughout Asia and the European continent.

P ersonal charm and fluency in French, Spanish, German, Russian, Latin and Greek made him a popular guest in the best social circles, including the court of Czar Alexander of Russia. During these years Poinsett developed a deep knowledge of, and interest in, science, agriculture and botany, and began his lifelong passion for finding and exchanging unusual plant specimens with fellow horticultural enthusiasts.

Joel Roberts Poinsett
(1779 - 1851)

SPECIAL ENVOY TO
ARGENTINA AND CHILE

SOUTH CAROLINA STATE LEGISLATOR

UNITED STATES CONGRESSMAN

FIRST AMBASSADOR TO MEXICO

PRESIDENT VAN BUREN'S
SECRETARY OF WAR

ADVISOR TO WEST POINT

FOUNDER OF THE
NATIONAL INSTITUTION FOR THE
PROMOTION OF SCIENCE (LATER THE
SMITHSONIAN INSTITUTION)

AND HORTICULTURAL ENTHUSIAST
RESPONSIBLE FOR THE "DISCOVERY"
OF POINSETTIAS

W hen he returned to the United States in 1811, Poinsett was acknowledged as one of the most sophisticated and erudite of all Americans, and, based on this reputation, President James Madison appointed him Special United States Envoy to Argentina and Chile. There he worked to convince the military junta in Buenos Aires to grant America "most favored nation" status, and became a valued military advisor to the President of Chile. He also helped the embryonic government organize a police force, establish a banking system and develop cotton and rice crops for export. In 1815, his assignment completed, Poinsett indulged his love of adventure and traveled more than 2,000 miles across the still untamed Western frontier.

A clear, concise, energetic public speaker with considerable personal magnetism, Poinsett was elected to the South Carolina State Legislature, and also served as head of the Board of Public Works, responsible for building all roads, dams, bridges and ports from 1817 through 1820.

I n 1820 he was elected to the United States Congress, and in his second term, President Andrew Jackson appointed him

POSTCARD, 1904.

the first United States Ambassador to Mexico. This was an extremely dangerous assignment, as the newly independent Republic was in the midst of a bloody civil war. Undaunted, Poinsett undertook discussions that eventually led to the U.S. purchase of Texas, and, indulging his passion for botany, introduced the American elm to Mexico, and exported Mimosa and hibiscus to the United States.

Fascinated by Mexico's natural beauty and archaeological treasures, Poinsett fearlessly braved bands of armed revolutionaries to roam the countryside in search of new plant species. In December, 1828 he took a serendipitous trip to Taxco where he "discovered" a dramatic-looking shrub with giant crimson flowers growing wild alongside the road and took cuttings to send back to his South Carolina plantation.

In 1829, he was re-elected to the South Carolina legislature. Eight years later, President Martin Van Buren appointed him Secretary of War, during which time he made major changes to West Point and oversaw the Second Seminole Indian War. In addition, Poinsett was the moving force behind the creation of a National Institution for the Promotion of Science, the objectives and scope of which were later adopted by the Smithsonian Institution.

By the time of his death in December 1851, a state park, major highway, hotel, private dining club, village and a multitude of Poinsett Streets and Avenues had been named in his honor. Yet despite his distinguished service to the United States and a myriad of personal accomplishments, Poinsett is remembered today for finding, cultivating and introducing a fiery red Mexican wild flower to America.

PHILOSOPHERS AND POETS have, since ancient times, created legends (stories about events in the past that some believe are true, but whose claims cannot be proven) to explain why plants look the way they do.

LEGEND HAS IT poinsettias were once insignifcant, mousy green shrubs that, due to a magical sequence of events, were transformed into breathtakingly beautiful ruby red stunners:

SOME BELIEVE the leaves turned the bright red color of blood in sympathy for a young woman who, separated from her one true love on Christmas Eve, died of a broken heart.

OTHERS CLAIM that when the Star of Bethlehem shot through the sky on the night Jesus was born, it turned the leaves the color of a fire's flames in its wake.

OR PERHAPS the metamorphosis occurred when Pepita, a poor peasant girl

began to cry and an angel, hearing the heartbreaking sound, floated to earth and asked, "Why do you weep?" Discovering the girl was sad because she didn't have money to buy a gift of value to offer the baby Jesus on Christmas Eve, the angel whispered, "A humble gift, offered in love, will be cherished as much as a grand one. Gather some of the weeds growing alongside the road. They will be your gift." As a puzzled Pepita bent to collect the scrawny-looking branches, her tears fell like rain and the ragged leaves burst into vibrant crimson blooms.

ANOTHER LEGEND proclaims the plants' leaves turned color when a young boy, miserable because he was too poor to buy a Christmas offering for the altar of a great Mexican cathedral, fell to his knees and asked for guidance. When he got up, the first red Flowers of the Holy Night sprang from the spot where he had knelt.

TREES AND EVERGREENS have played an integral part in winter ceremonies for more than 5,000 years because people believed powerful gods lived inside them. Although these gods were invisible, their voices could be heard when the wind whistled through the leaves and their life force could be seen when a branch broke and sap, like blood, flowed from the limb.

So in winter when the sun shone less and less each day (a sure sign that the Sun god was dying), people all over the world, from Scandinavia to Egypt and from China to the Americas, turned to these leafy green gods to help them revive the sun. In every corner of the globe, the winter ceremonies to cure the god included trees and evergreens. And they worked! Afterwards, the evil forces that darkened the sky subsided, the Sun god's power was restored, and spring returned to earth.

ON DECEMBER 24TH the Egyptians wove evergreens, pine cones, rosemary and laurel together to make a wreath which was hung over the front door to frighten away the gods of darkness. Priests decorated date palms and lit candles at a midnight service to warm the ailing god.

These rituals were rewarded when, at dawn on December 25th, the Sun god was reborn in the morning sky and people shouted in joy, "The light of the world has returned."

SATURNALIA, the Birth-Day of the Unconquered Sun, was celebrated by the ancient Romans in late December. During this time Romans exchanged the traditional gift of a bough of greenery from the groves of the goddess Strenia. These *strenae*, the Roman word for "presents," were often combined with jars of honey and gold to guarantee the recipient a new year filled with sweetness and prosperity.

IN ANCIENT JAPAN, evergreen pine boughs and bamboo were given as good luck charms to ensure happiness and long life in the new year.

THE CELTS brought sweet-smelling hawthorns inside during December believing that when the frozen gods living inside thawed out, they would express their gratitude by bestowing good luck and long life on the family.

POSTCARD, 1908.

Paul Ecke Ranch, Encinitas, California

Care &
Cultivation

"No occupation is so delightful to me
as the culture of the earth,
and no culture comparable to that
of the garden."

Thomas Jefferson (1743-1826)

Buyer Beware!

◆ Plants, like melons, can be over ripe.
Examine the *cyathia,* the tiny yellow
or green berries in the center of the *bracts.*
If they are tight, the plant is still fresh.

◆ Ask when the protective paper, mesh or
plastic sleeve was put on. If it has been
more than a couple of days, the foliage
may be damaged.

◆ Rush poinsettias indoors if it's freezing
outside. They wilt if exposed, even for
a few minutes, to temperatures below
50 degrees.

*f*OR

PICTURE
PERFECT
POINSETTIAS:

**Poinsettias
LOVE to be pampered!**

1. Feed plants with a high nitrogen fertilizer every two weeks.

2. Mist every other day.

3. Offer tiny sips of tepid water every other day.

4. Place in a draft-free environment with constant 60 to 70 degree temperatures and six hours of indirect, filtered sunlight.

LONGWOOD GARDENS, PENNSYLVANIA, 1992.

*"When the world wearies and society ceases to satisfy,
there is always the garden."*

VICTORIAN VERSE

TROUBLE-FREE POINSETTIAS. COTTON FABRIC, 1990.

Rx For A Fading Beauty

Holidays stress out plants as well as people.
If your poinsettias start looking bedraggled, don't despair.
Grab a cup of eggnog, and read on to find a remedy:

SYMPTOM:
Foliage is rotted, wilted, bleached out. Plant turns yellow and drops its leaves.
DIAGNOSIS:
Too much water.
RX:
Let dry out between waterings.

SYMPTOM:
Leaf tips turn brown, yellow. New growth is stunted. Begins to drop buds.
DIAGNOSIS:
Not enough humidity.
RX:
Mist daily.

SYMPTOM:
Plant stems are limp. Leaves have yellow and brown spots and curl under.
DIAGNOSIS:
Not enough water.
RX:
Take a wild guess!

SYMPTOM:
Leaves are discolored, tips turn brown and die.
DIAGNOSIS:
Not enough bright light.
RX:
Relocate to a spot with six hours of bright light a day.

SYMPTOM:
Leaves turn yellow, fall off. No new flowers appear.
DIAGNOSIS:
Sudden changes in temperature.
RX:
Move away from drafts.

SYMPTOM:
New growth dies back. Stems are soft and dark.
DIAGNOSIS:
Uh, oh. Root rot, which prevents the root system from absorbing water, has set in.
RX:
Consult a plant doctor. You may need a prescription.

Paul Ecke Ranch

A WORD ABOUT PESTS

Poinsettias are pest-free in the wild, but indoors are subject to whiteflies, fungus, spider mites and mealy bugs. What to do? Carefully carry the infested plant to the kitchen sink and, treating it like a precious piece of crystal, gently wash the leaves and stems with a mild detergent. Try singing Christmas carols while patting the leaves dry...it can't hurt!

Greetings

GREEN PLANTS LIKE
POINSETTIAS HAVE PLAYED
A PIVOTAL ROLE IN
DECEMBER CEREMONIES FOR
THOUSANDS OF YEARS.
FOR EXAMPLE, IN DECEMBER
THE DRUIDS, WHO
CONSIDERED HOLLY SACRED,
SCATTERED IT ALL AROUND
TO PROTECT AGAINST
WITCHES, BAD DREAMS,
THE EVIL EYE AND
DISLOCATED BONES.
ANCIENT GERMANIC AND
BRITISH TRIBES ALSO
USED HOLLY IN THEIR WINTER
CEREMONIES AND INSTEAD OF
DISCARDING IT AFTERWARDS
(TANTAMOUNT TO THROWING
AWAY PROSPERITY AND
GOOD HEALTH),
THE LEAVES WERE
BREWED INTO A BITTER TEA
AND USED TO CURE WINTER
COLDS, COLIC, MEASLES
AND WHOOPING COUGH.

Life, Liberty & the Pursuit of Happiness

Don't be cruel. Resist the temptation to discard poinsettias when they loose their looks. In tropical and subtropical zones, poinsettias *like* being put out to pasture. Many, haphazardly tossed alongside roadways in Hawaii, Europe and the continental United States, now tower 12 to 15 feet high. Retired to the backyard, they will enjoy a second career as a stunningly beautiful, informal hedge, and if planted in slightly acidic, well-drained soil against a sunny wall in a sheltered corner, most won't even require special care.

NO NIGHT-LIGHTS, PLEASE

Flowering is directly related to the intensity, quantity, and amount of light a plant receives. Cacti, succulents, annuals and gray-leafed specimens with fleshy cell walls and tough exteriors need lots of light to bloom. Others, like philodendrons, with larger, thinner-textured leaves thrive in low light. Poinsettias (and chrysanthemums), are extremely light sensitive and will refuse to bud if even a tiny shaft of artificial light from a night-light or passing car casts a shadow on their leaves. To flower, they *must* be cloaked in total darkness for 14 hours a day from late September to early October.

1907 POSTCARD OF A 23 FOOT HIGH POINSETTIA IN HOLLYWOOD, CALIFORNIA.

To Relocate Your Seasonal Dazzler:

1. Stop watering when poinsettias drop their leaves.
2. Move to a semi-shaded window and water once a month.
3. Perform cosmetic surgery in late March or early April. Cut stems back to 4 inches, then place in a warm, shady spot.
4. In summer, repot in new soil: combine 2 parts all-purpose loam, 2 parts sand and 1 part peat moss. Place in a sunny window and water sparingly.
5. After the last frost, set poinsettias outdoors in full sun. Prune to prevent legginess, keep soil evenly moist.
6. Bring indoors in September.
7. Place in a dark spot, like a closet, for at least 14 hours a day through October.
8. When new growth sprouts, water and feed once a week.

POSTCARD, 1901(above), LONGWOOD GARDENS, 1991 (below).

Longwood Gardens – Photo: Larry Albee

Monet

Stippled with pink and peach, this cream-colored poinsettia, inspired by the delicate brushwork of the French impressionist painter Claude Monet, won a blue ribbon in The Society of American Florists New Varieties Competition, the floral industry's highest honor.

Dreaming of a *white* Christmas?

Growers began experimenting with poinsettias' color to broaden their appeal. A difficult and time-consuming task, only 1 in 100 are deemed good enough for further color experimentation. Some of the colors that finally made it out of the greenhouse and into the marketplace are:

Color	Year
White	1945
Pink	1964
Pink & White	1969
Jingle Bells (red with pink flecks)	1973
Salmon	1988
Monet	1993

Paul Ecke Ranch Encinitas California

Every Color, Shape & Size

Aided by growth retardants and scientific breeding techniques, there are now 6 families and 30 poinsettia *cultivars*, from brilliant red, a cherished fixture on the Christmas party circuit, to bright white, a favorite at December weddings.

These Pygmalian-like transformations over the last 50 years have not been easy. First, growers had to reduce the overall size of the tall, gangly wildflower from 3 meters (10 feet) to 45 to 60cm (1½ to 2 feet). Next, the plants had to be coaxed into flowering earlier and more prolifically. And finally, breeders struggled to retrain the plants which had the nasty habit of dropping their leaves as soon as they left the greenhouse.

Perhaps the most awesome adaptations are the teeny two-inch miniatures and bonsais that thrive in a thimbleful of soil. A European favorite, these self sufficient poinsettias even water themselves through a string that dangles from their roots to the bottom of a plastic cube filled with water.

Lemon Drop, as yummy-looking as its namesake, a lemony-tasting candy, was cultivated to extend poinsettias' season into November and the Thanksgiving holiday.

A lush apricot-colored poinsettia is being specifically developed to harmonize with Southwestern and Mediterranean decors.

Paul Ecke Ranch, Encinitas, California

Fame & Fortune

*"Fame sometimes hath created
something of nothing."*

Thomas Fuller (1608 - 1661)

A New Custom

Dr. Poinsett regularly sent seeds, cuttings and bulbs to a network of people who shared his passion for gardening. As fate would have it, one of the poinsettia cuttings he sent from Mexico went to John Bartram in Philadelphia. Bartram's grand-daughter's husband, Colonel Carr, awed by the unusual plants' brilliant, spectacular blooms submitted them to the 1829 Exposition of the Pennsylvania Horticultural Society. The flowers were an overnight sensation.

Then Bartram sent one of *his* cuttings to Robert Buist, a prominent Philadelphia nurseryman and florist. Buist, intrigued by the plant's unique coloring, began growing it in *his* greenhouse. Slowly it dawned on him that the green leafed plants that bloomed red at Christmastime might have real commercial possibilities.

Poinsettia Euphorbia

FLEURS EXOTIQUES BY CLAUDE VINCON, 1962.

Over the next 20 years, Buist offered *"Euphorbia poinsettia"* for sale in Philadelphia and New York, and they became a red-hot best-seller. Nurseries all over the United States and Europe, particularly in Scotland and England, wrote begging for cuttings. Thus, a new Christmas custom was born.

CHRISTMASTIME AT THE WASHINGTON MARKET IN NEW YORK CITY, *HARPER'S WEEKLY*, SEPTEMBER 1878.

THE CULTIVATION OF A BEST-SELLER

Paul Ecke Ranch Encinitas, California

"Diligence is the mother of good luck."
BENJAMIN FRANKLIN (1706-1790)

POINSETTIAS' PLACE IN HISTORY as *the* Christmas flower is largely due to Albert Ecke, a German immigrant to Hollywood, California, who in 1902 began to raise vegetables, gladiolas and chrysanthemums for sale in the local markets. Business was booming in December, 1906, when his son Paul hiked up the hill above their ranch on a whim, picked an armful of bright red wildflowers, and carried them down to the family's flower stand on Sunset Boulevard. Customers fell in love with the festive red and green flowers, and by the end of the holiday season poinsettias were the most sought-after cut flower in Southern California. Dazzled by the demand, the Eckes gradually abandoned their other crops to devote full time to the genetic research, breeding, hybridizing and distribution of poinsettias.

THE BUDDING BUSINESS relocated to Encinitas, California in 1920, and, with the development of a new poinsettia which could be sold as a potted plant, the Eckes stopped raising cut flowers in order to produce field-grown *mother plants* which could be shipped in railroad box cars to greenhouses throughout the United States. By 1963, a heartier plant capable of surviving longer periods of time in lower temperatures was developed, and poinsettias began to enjoy worldwide popularity as a Yuletide tradition.

PAUL ECKE, SR. (1895-1991)

TODAY, the holiday dynasty grows poinsettias in California on 35 acres of greenhouses and in Denmark. Together these facilities produce 90% of all poinsettias sold in the United States, Europe and the Pacific Rim.

THE STATE DINING ROOM IN THE WHITE HOUSE, DECEMBER, 1970.

The Richard Nixon Library & Birthplace

THE FIRST LADY of the United States personally supervises the holiday decorations for the White House, and in doing so, helps reinforce certain holiday traditions (if something is good enough for the White House, it *must* be OK for the rest of the country). And every year since 1960 (when Mamie Eisenhower decorated 26 trees, including one in the laundry room) lush displays of poinsettias, the all-American holiday plant, have played an important part in Christmas at the White House.

Bush Presidential Materials Project

Paul Ecke Ranch Encinitas, California

They're Number One

In 1986, poinsettias gently nudged chrysanthemums aside to become the number one best-selling potted plant in the United States. Remember, this is despite the fact that poinsettias are only sold during a two month period, while their competitors have twelve months to tally up impressive sales statistics.

Year	Plants Sold
1959	7,000,000
1979	28,000,000
1986	37,000,000
1996	71,000,000

Good Timing:

The Franciscan priests living near Taxco, Mexico in the 1600s were the first to use poinsettias in a Christian ceremony. The flowers, in full, glorious bloom during the Fiesta of Santa Pesebre made a colorful addition to their nativity procession. To this day, poinsettias play an important part in the Guatemalan Indians' December festivities.

*"Fresh as the flowers
may all
your pleasures be…"*

<small>VICTORIAN VERSE</small>

Americans wholeheartedly
embraced poinsettias,
and within a decade of their
introduction into
the United States, the flame
red flower was a beloved

Christmas Classic

and its unique star-shaped
profile began appearing on
Christmas cards and other
holiday items alongside
thousand-year-old traditions
like holly and jolly
old St. Nick.

THE 1920s

Just A Bit O' Christmas

THE 1950s

A very Merry Christmas.

The 1910s

SOME THINGS NEVER CHANGE

"...everywhere may be seen...well-laden tables; luxurious abundance is found in the houses of the rich, but also in the houses of the poor; better food than usual is put upon the table. The impulse to spend seizes everyone... People are not only generous to themselves, but also to their fellow men.

A stream of presents pours itself out on all sides...The Kalends festival* banishes all that is connected with toil, and allows men to give themselves up to undisturbed enjoyment."

LIBANIUS
4TH CENTURY, GREECE

*A new year's celebration in honor of Janus, the god of all beginnings.

A CHRISTMAS GREETING
To my Daughter

THE 1930s

 GIFTWRAP, THE 1960s

A Christmas Greeting
TO A MIGHTY NICE NURSE

The 1940s

POINSETTIAS = DECEMBER

Smithsonian Institution, Archives of American Gardens, Horticulture Services Collection

Yosemite Concession Services • Photo: Keith S Walklet

THESE PHOTOGRAPHS COULD HAVE BEEN TAKEN ANYTIME DURING THE YEAR, BUT THE PRESENCE OF THOSE DISTINCTIVE RED *bracts* AMID THE OPULENCE OF THE SMITHSONIAN AND THE RUSTIC CHARM OF THE AHWAHNEE HOTEL AT YOSEMITE "TELLS" US THEY WERE SNAPPED IN DECEMBER.

FLOWER POWER

Poinsettias are commercially grown
in all 50 of the United States
(yes, even Alaska).

TOP TEN STATES WHERE
POINSETTIAS ARE
GROWN & NUMBER SOLD*

1.	California	7.8 million
2.	Ohio	4.2 million
3.	North Carolina	4.1 million
4.	Pennsylvania	3.8 million
5.	Michigan	3.4 milllion
6.	Florida	3.4 million
7.	New York	3.1 million
8.	Texas	3.0 million
9.	New Jersey	2.2 million
10.	Wisconsin	1.8 million

*Source: United States Department of Agriculture
Floriculture Crops Report, 1994.

SOUTHERN CALIFORNIANS ARE TREATED
TO A SNEAK PREVIEW OF NEW SUBSPECIES
AND *CULTIVARS* (CULTIVATED VARIETIES),
LIKE WINTER ROSE™ CURLY™ RED,
WHEN PAUL ECKE RANCH TEST MARKETS
"NEW AND IMPROVED" HYBRIDS IN THE
REGION EACH YEAR. IT TOOK 30 YEARS
TO COAX THIS PARTICULARLY STUBBORN
BEAUTY TO CHANGE ITS FORM FROM A 6
FOOT TALL CUT FLOWER TO A LUSH,
COMPACT POTTED PLANT.

An (International) Star is Born

Prior to 1965, the European market for poinsettias was confined to cut flowers. But with the opening of a production facility in Denmark the worldwide sales of potted poinsettias soared. The plants' international standing received another boost in 1991 with the formation of the Poinsettia Growers Association. With 600 members in more than 40 countries actively working to improve the marketing, education and research programs of growers worldwide, it's no wonder poinsettias are *the* (international) December flower.

National Poinsettia Day

In 1991, the United States Congress declared December 12th National Poinsettia Day to commemorate the life of Dr. Joel Roberts Poinsett, who died on this day in 1851. Poinsett was responsible for introducing Americans to the enduring beauty of poinsettias.

December Birthdays

"Guide me in proper ways so that I may live a long,
happy life, for this is my birthday."

HINDU SONG

Courtesy of the Hallmark Archives, Hallmark Cards, Inc.

POSTCARD, 1906.

FOUR THOUSAND YEARS AGO an Egyptian Pharaoh celebrated the day he was born at the first Birth-Day party ever. The Persians, universally renowned as confectioners, improved on the party idea by adding a sweet cake, but only royal males warranted the treat, as the Birth-Days of women, children, and commoners just weren't important enough to record. Worshippers of the moon goddess Artemis placed candles on the cake, believing the flames would keep evil spirits at bay and the smoke would carry their prayers to the goddess in heaven.

DURING THE MIDDLE AGES people wore jewelry encrusted with the gemstone associated with the month of their birth to thwart demons and ensure the wearer good fortune. The birthstone for December babies is a ruby.

EACH OF THE TWELVE MONTHS was also paired with a flower. In December, a floral gift of narcissus was said to bring good luck to a birthday boy or girl. But by the 1940s the public's passion for poinsettias made them the preferred flower for the outspoken, optimistic (Sagittarius: November 23-December 20) ambitious, and witty (Capricorn: December 21- January 19) people born in December.

Longwood Gardens in Pennsylvania, 1987.

Poinsettia
Potpourri

*"…flowers have a
mysterious and subtle influence
upon the feelings…"*

Henry Ward Beecher (1813-1887)

Ꮐoing to the 𝒟ogs?

"Raymond Loewy, the industrial designer, sent his office boy over to the Public Library recently, with instructions to borrow some prints of holly and poinsettia.
(We don't know what sort of industrial design Mr. Loewy needed these for.)
The office boy was back in no time, with three pictures. One was of a sprig of holly.
*The other two were of a **pointer** and a **setter**."*

The New Yorker "The Talk of the Town", June 29, 1940.

Poinsettia motifs adorn all sorts of personal apparel, from blouses to boxer shorts, belts, necklaces, earrings, handbags, bracelets, nightgowns, skirts, ribbons, wristwatch bands, shirts, socks, shoes, robes...and, the hats worn over the years by Christmas revelers.

Christmas Shopping, 1995.

A Merry Christmas to you

CHRISTMAS CARD, 1912.

$\mathcal{T}$ie-ing $\mathcal{O}$ne $\mathcal{O}$n

Roy Larson developed a passion for neckties in the fourth grade. Then as a North Carolina State University Professor Emeritus he performed poinsettia research. So, it logically follows that 60 out of the 500 ties in his collection feature the festive plants.

Courtesy of Roy & Darlyne Larson

Paul Ecke Ranch

In December, 1920 *Good Housekeeping* suggested a holiday party with handmade red crepe paper poinsettia shaped invitations which, when the guests arrived, could be turned into an ice-breaker game:

"Invitations – With each note of invitation enclose part of a stemless poinsettia prepared in this way: Cut poinsettias from red crepe paper in a convenient size for half of one flower to fit in each envelope. Paste the poinsettias on white notepaper and cut out around the petals, then cut each poinsettia half in two, in an uneven line. On the notepaper side of each piece of poinsettia write the following verse:

This gay red flower cut in two
Will bring your partner
straight to you,
If in your search you
do not cease
Until you find the other piece.

Courtesy of the Hubbard Twins

After all the guests arrive, explain that they are to match their pieces of poinsettia to find partners for the evening."

By the 1950s ordinary items like the plastic covers used by dry cleaners and the brown paper bags from the grocery were being festively adorned with poinsettias' distinctive profile. In 1978, pretty potted poinsettias even made it onto the football field when Navy played Brigham Young in San Diego's first Holiday Bowl. Could sheets, towels, comforters and china be far behind?

Serendipity

Had Dr. Poinsett lived just a few miles north of his home in Charleston, South Carolina, poinsettias might never have decorated quilts or tea cups because the cooler temperatures there would have prevented the cuttings he brought back from Mexico from turning red. And, without their brilliant, distinctive color, the plants probably would have languished in obscurity for another 200 plus years.

Colorful poinsettias decorate a cotton quilt believed to have been appliqued in Maine, circa 1830.

Replacements, Ltd. Greensboro, North Carolina 1-800/737-5223

For a Convivial Holiday Meal:
Holiday Bouquet by Schumann (top), Poinsettia by Block (left), Noel by Royalty (right).

Pretty Picture Postcards of Poinsettias

ALL CORRESPONDENCE prior to 1865 required ink, stationery, a pen, paper, an envelope, sealing wax and a seal to close the envelope. Heinrich von Stephan thought this a tedious bore and devised a solution: a card that could be posted without an envelope. In 1870, the British government decided they liked the idea and issued "postal leaflets" which sold 76 million in the first year.

THE POSTMASTER General of the United States, impressed with the success and convenience of the British cards asked Congress in 1872 to issue similar cards. In 1898, Congress gave private companies the right to publish postcards which could be sent for the same rate as the government's postcards.

IN 1903, France became the first country to sanction a two-sided postcard: one side for the address, message and stamp, the other for a picture. American printers quickly followed suit. Poinsettias were often added to stock color photographs to transform postcards into a unique, attractive (and very popular) holiday greeting.

POSTCARD, 1912.

POST CARD

FOR CORRESPONDENCE

WORLD'S
PANAMA-
PACIFIC
FOR ADDRESS
EXPOSITION
1915

SAN FRANCISCO
DEC 25
9-30 AM
1914

Mrs. W. Trumbull
3916 - 22 nd St.

Peter

To wish you a very
Happy Christmas.

POSTCARD, 1910.

A
friend's
Greeting to you
on Christmas-day

CHRISTMAS
GREETINGS

THE TETON MOUNTAINS

IDAHO
THE
GEM STATE

JAN. 1ST

HAPPY NEW YEAR

POSTCARD, 1912.

POINSETTIA *Trees*

THE POINSETTIA TREES IN THE "CASTLE" AT THE SMITHSONIAN IN WASHINGTON, D.C., 1995 (ABOVE) AND IN THE KROHN CONSERVATORY IN CINCINNATI, OHIO, 1984 (BELOW).

THE TERM "CHRISTMAS TREE" first appeared in 1830 in a York, Pennsylvania newspaper. The article, which described a fund-raiser sponsored by some society ladies, enthused that for six cents visitors to the Yuletide bazaar would be treated to the sight of a charmingly decorated "Christmas Tree".

THE FIRST CHRISTMAS TREE LOT was set up in 1851 by a farmer from the Catskill mountains. When Mark Carr told his wife he was going to cut down two wagonloads of pines from the backyard, bundle them onto a ship, and travel 80 miles down the Hudson River to sell them in New York City, she laughed. Nevertheless, he perservered, and to his delight, sold them all in a single day. Forty years later, the tree lots in New York City sold more than 200,000 holiday trees, and Christmas tree lots were commonplace throughout the United States.

POINSETTIA TREES WERE FIRST SET UP AT THE EMBARCADERO CENTERS AND HYATT REGENCY HOTEL IN SAN FRANCISCO, CALIFORNIA IN 1974. EVERY YEAR UNTIL 1992 FIVE 20-FOOT-TALL, SPECIALLY CONSTRUCTED, PYRAMID-SHAPED STRUCTURES WERE FILLED WITH 600 RED AND WHITE POINSETTIAS. A REMARKABLE SIGHT, PEOPLE TRAVELED FROM ALL OVER THE SAN FRANCISCO BAY AREA TO FEAST THEIR EYES ON THESE UNUSUAL, SPECTACULAR-LOOKING CHRISTMAS TREES.

IT'S *Tradition*

DOES FAMILIARITY BREED CONTEMPT? CAN THERE BE TOO MUCH OF A GOOD THING? IN A 1991 ARTICLE ABOUT THE PROS AND CONS OF POINSETTIAS, JON CARROLL OPINED, *"THE POINSETTIA IS TO THE PLANT WORLD WHAT THE FRUITCAKE IS TO THE FOOD WORLD. LITERALLY MILLIONS OF BOTH ARE GIVEN AS GIFTS EVERY HOLIDAY SEASON, NOT BECAUSE ANYONE WANTS THEM OR NEEDS THEM, BUT BECAUSE IT'S TRADITION."* TO THIS, CONNIE BALLARD, ON BEHALF OF POINSETTIA LOVERS THE WORLD OVER RETORTED, *"SOME THINGS ARE FOREVER. TURKEYS GO WITH THANKSGIVING. POINSETTIAS GO WITH CHRISTMAS. TRADITIONS DON'T GO OUT OF STYLE. THAT'S WHY THEY'RE CALLED TRADITIONS."* ENOUGH SAID.

ACKNOWLEDGMENTS

Bouquets to the following for their kind permission to reproduce images in this book:

Alexander Henry Collection: Endpapers
Bush Presidential Materials Project: Page 42
California Academy of Sciences: Pages 10, 40
Concord Fabrics, Inc.: Page 61
Domestications: Page 56
Dover Publications, Inc.: Pages 23, 40
Paul Ecke Ranch: Cover, Title Pages & 12, 18-19, 22, 27-30, 33, 36-39, 41-43, 47-48, 55, 60
The Embarcadero Center: Page 60
The Farnsworth Art Museum: Page 56
The Hallmark Archives: Pages 44-45, 49
Hats on Post: Page 52

Janice & Joyce Hubbard: Page 55
Juan Antonia Fernandez-Oronoz: Page 13
Roy & Darlyne Larson: Page 54
Longwood Gardens: Pages 30, 32, 35, 50-51
Lyons Ltd. Antique Prints: Pages 8-9, 14-15, 17
Museum of the City of New York: Pages 40, 45, 53
The Richard Nixon Library & Birthplace: Page 42
Replacements, Ltd.: Page 57
Smithsonian Institution: Pages 20, 46, 60
Strawberry Press: Page 11
Susan's Store Room: Pages 12, 26
Yosemite Concession Services: Page 46

BIBLIOGRAPHY

Allan, Mea. *Weeds*. New York: The Viking Press, 1978.

Ballard, Connie and Jon Carrol. "Return of the Poinsettia." *San Francisco Chronicle*, December 4, 1991.

Black, Marvin. "Hardy Euphorbias for the Border." *Pacific Horticulture*, May 1984.

Bonar, Ann. *Plants to Grow in the Home*. New York: Galahad Books, 1976.

Brown, Dennis A. *The Encyclopedia Botanica*. New York: The Dial Press, 1978.

Census of Agriculture: Floriculture Crops Report, Washington D.C., April 1993.

Chalmers, Rena. *The Great American Christmas Almanac*, New York: Viking Studio Books, 1988.

Coffin, Tristram Potter. *The Book of Christmas Folklore*. New York: The Seabury Press, 1973.

Croizat, Leon. *De Euphorbio Antiquorum Atque Officinarum: A Study of Succulent Euphorbiae*. New York: Eric Walther Library, 1934.

Crowson, E. Thomas. "Senor Poinsett and the Chilean Revolutionaries." *South Carolina History Illustrated*, Volume 1, Number 4, 1970.

Dickey, Thomas, Vance Muse and Henry Wiencek. *The God-Kings of Mexico*. Chicago, Illinois: Tree Communications, Inc., 1982.

Ecke, Paul Jr., O.A. Matkin and David E. Hartley. *The Poinsettia Manual*. Encinitas, California: Paul Ecke Poinsettias, 1990.

"Poinsettia Party for the Holiday Season, by Elaine." *Good HouseKeeping*. December 1920.

Heilman, Grace W. and Bernard S. Levin, Editors. *Calendar of Joel R. Poinsett Papers*. Philadelphia: The Gilpin Library of The Historical Society of Pennsylvania, 1941.

Hildebrand, Norbert A. *A New Look at Christmas Decorations*. Milwaukee: The Bruce Publishing Company.

Hotchkiss, Joseph W. *A Family Christmas*. New York: The Reader's Digest Association, 1984.

Ickis, Marguerite. *The Book of Festival Holidays*. New York: Dodd, Mead & Company, 1964.

Klamkin, Marian. *Picture Postcards*. New York: Dodd, Mead & Company, 1974.

Kramer, Jack. *1000 Beautiful Plants and How to Grow Them*. New York: William Morrow & Company, Inc., 1969.

The National Cyclopaedia of American Biography Being the History of the United States, Volume VI. Ann Arbor, Michigan: University Microfilms, 1967.

Rippy, J. Fred. *Joel R. Poinsett, Versatile American*. Durham, North Carolina: Duke University Press, 1935.

Ross, Shirley. *First Aid for House Plants*. New York: McGraw-Hill Book Company, 1976.

Rowley, Gordon. "The Succulent Spurges: Landmarks in Early History." *The Euphorbia Journal*, Volume II. Mill Valley, California: Strawberry Press, 1984.

Sechrist, Elizabeth Hough. *Christmas Everywhere: A Book of Christmas Customs of Many Lands*. Philadelphia: Macrae Smith Company, 1962.

Shakey, Karen. *Ortho's Complete Guide to Successful Houseplants*. San Francisco: 1984.

Shaver Houghton, Claire. *Green Immigrants: The Plants That Transformed America*. New York: Harcourt Brace Jovanovich, 1978.

Vaillant, G. C. *Aztecs of Mexico*. New York: Doubleday & Company, Inc., 1944.

Weiser, Francis X. *The Christmas Book*. New York: Harcourt, Brace and Company.

Willard, B. L. "Joel Poinsett, the Politician." *The State Magazine*. December 9, 1984.

ENAMEL PIN, 1994.

Index

INQUIRIES

- ◆ Know an interesting poinsettia fact?
- ◆ Have an unusual poinsettia "thing"?
- ◆ Want a copy of the curriculum guide based on *Poinsettias* for 2nd through 5th grades? If so, please contact:

WATERS EDGE PRESS
98 Main Street #527
Tiburon, CA 94920
(415) 435-2837
FAX: (415) 435-2404
EMAIL: books@watersedgepress.com
WEBSITE: www.watersedgepress.com